The Complete Oxford PAT guide
Part I: Notes and Formulae

RJ Beresford

2020 Edition

Content by RJ Beresford

First Printing: July 2018

Cover and book design by Vir Publishers

ISBN: 979-8634235394

Contents

Introduction

The test consists of maths and physics questions, the maths questions are generally straight forward, but usually require a sound logical approach to the problem, and not just knowledge from the A Level specification. The physics questions are often considered harder compared to the maths questions since the application of physics theory can become challenging.

Note: Many students often do not apply since they think their GCSE grades are 'not good enough', but this should not be the case. Oxford admits students based on their potential and passion, and though GCSE grades are a factor in the application they are not as important as the PAT or interview.

The application process: UCAS -> PAT -> Interview -> Offer -> A-Levels

Physics: With Physics, Oxford sets a threshold cutoff score where only those above are admitted to interview (unless there are extenuating circumstances). The cutoff is determined by the paper difficulty. Oxford has published cutoffs and statistics for past years on their website, under the PAT section. Students have 2-3 interviews over the course of their stay. The interview is also extremely important but tutors are now looking for passion for the subject as well as potential (a quality that cannot be gauged in a written assessment).

Engineering Science and Material Sciences: Both are a little more lenient on the PAT and consider the interview highly, it has been shown in past years that to pass to the offer stage, your interview score must be higher than 7/9 (Source: Engineering FOI request). BUT the PAT is still an extremely important element of the application and should not be overlooked to be any less of a contributing factor than the interview since the process is very much a holistic one, taking into account GCSEs, A Level predictions, your UCAS form, references, PAT and interview.

Part I of the guide aims to summarise AS Level Physics and elements of the A2 Physics course in order to better prepare you for the Oxford Physics Aptitude Test as well as the Interview. In order to succeed in the PAT and Interview a solid basis of knowledge is required. Mechanics, waves and electricity are the three most important physics topics, whilst maths questions range from geometry to statistics.

Chapter 1

Syllabus (as of 2020)

1.1 Maths

Elementary mathematics:

Knowledge of elementary mathematics, in particular topics in arithmetic, geometry including coordinate geometry, and probability, will be assumed. Questions may require the manipulation of mathematical expressions in a physical context.

Algebra:

Knowledge of the properties of polynomials, including the solution of quadratics either using a formula or by factorising. Graph sketching including the use of differentiation to find stationary points. Transformations of variables. Solutions to inequalities. Elementary trigonometry including relationships between sine, cosine and tangent (sum and difference formulae will be stated if required). Properties of logarithms and exponentials and how to combine logarithms, e.g. log(a) + log(b) = log(ab) . Knowledge of the formulae for the sum of arithmetic and geometric progressions to n (or infinite) terms. Use of the binomial expansion for expressions using only positive integer values of n, such as:

$$(a + bx)^n$$

Calculus:

Differentiation and integration of polynomials including fractional and negative powers. Differentiation to find the slope of a curve, and the location of maxima and minima. Integration as the reverse of differentiation and as finding the area under a curve. Simplifying integrals by symmetry arguments including use of the properties of even and odd functions (where an even function has f(x)= f(-x), an odd function has f(-x)= - f(x)).

1.2 Physics

Mechanics:

Distance, velocity, speed, acceleration, and the relationships between them, e.g. velocity as the rate of change of distance with time, acceleration as rate of change of velocity with time. Understand the difference between vector quantities (e.g. velocity) and scalar quantities (e.g. speed). Knowledge and use of equations such as speed = distance / time, acceleration = change in velocity / time or the SUVAT equations. Interpretation of graphs, e.g. force-distance, distance-time, velocity-time graphs and what the gradient of a curve or area underneath a curve represents. Response of a system to multiple forces; Newton's laws of motion; know the difference between weight ($= mg$) and mass; vector addition of forces. Circular motion including equations for centripetal force ($F = m\omega^2 r$ or $F = mv^2/r$) and acceleration ($a = v^2/r$ or $a =^2 r$). The meaning of the terms friction, air resistance and terminal velocity and how they can be calculated. Levers (including taking moments about a point on an object), pulleys (including calculating the tension in a rope or the overall motion in a system of ropes and pulleys) and other simple machines combining levers, springs and pulleys. Springs, including knowledge of Hooke's law (Force = - kx) and stored potential energy ($= 1/2kx^2$). Kinetic energy ($= 1/2mv^2$) and gravitational potential energy ($= mgh$ in a constant gravitational field) and their inter-conversion; what other forms of energy exist (e.g. thermal, sound). Conservation of energy and momentum (=mass x velocity); power (= energy transfer/time) and work (= force x distance moved in direction of force).

Waves and optics:

An understanding of the terms longitudinal and transverse waves; and that waves transfer energy without net movement of matter. Be able to define the amplitude, frequency, period, wavelength and speed of a wave. Knowledge and use of formulae for the wave speed = wavelength x frequency and frequency = 1 / period (with units of hertz, Hz). Basic properties of the electromagnetic spectrum, e.g. identify and correctly order parts of the spectrum by wavelength or frequency (radio waves, microwaves, IR, visible light, UV, X rays and gamma rays) and the nature and properties of electromagnetic waves (transverse, travel at the speed of light in a vacuum). Description of reflection at plane mirrors, where the angle of incidence (the angle between the incident ray and the normal) = angle of reflection (angle between the reflected ray and the normal). Refraction, including the definition of refractive index (n) as the ratio of the speed of light in a vacuum to the speed of light in a material and Snell's law $n_1 sin_1 = n_2 sin_2$. Elementary properties of prisms and optical fibres including total internal reflection, where total internal reflection occurs at an angle c when $sin_c = n_2/n_1$ Qualitative understanding of how interference, diffraction and standing waves can occur.

Electricity and magnetism:

Understanding of the terms current (= charge / time), voltage (potential difference = energy / charge), charge, resistance (= voltage / current) and links to energy and power (power = voltage x current, power = energy / time). Knowledge of transformers, including how the number of turns on the primary and secondary coils affect the voltage and current. Understanding circuit diagrams including batteries, wires, resistors, filament lamps, diodes, capacitors, light dependent resistors and thermistors. Knowledge of current, voltage and resistance rules for series and parallel circuits. Knowledge of the force between two point charges ($F = kQ_1Q_2/r^2$ (where k is a constant)) and on a point charge in a constant electric field (Force = charge x electric field). Understanding that current is a flow of electrons; the photoelectric effect, where photoelectrons are emitted if they are given sufficient energy to overcome the work function of the material, and how to find the energy of accelerated electron beams (energy = charge x potential difference).

Natural world:

Atomic structure; that atoms consist of protons, neutrons and electrons, definition of the atomic number, Bohr model of the atom. Basic knowledge of bodies in our Solar System, including planets, moons, comets and asteroids. (Name and relative positions of the planets should be known but detailed knowledge of their physical parameters is not required). Know what is meant by the phrases 'phases of the moon' and 'eclipses' and how the position of the observer on the Earth affects their view of these events. Knowledge of circular orbits under gravity including orbital speed, radius, period, centripetal acceleration, and gravitational centripetal force. This may include equating the force between two masses due to gravity ($F = GM_1M_2/r^2$) to centripetal force of a smaller body orbiting a larger body ($F = m\omega^2 r$ or $F = mv^2/r$) and use of centripetal acceleration ($a = v^2/r$ or $a = \omega^2 r$). Understanding of the terms satellites; geostationary and polar orbits.

Problem solving:

Problems may be set which require problem solving based on information provided rather than knowledge about a topic.

Chapter 2

Physics Formulae

Mechanics (All suvat eq. are required):

$$F = ma$$

$$s = ut$$

$$W = Fd$$

$$T = mg$$

$$Power = Fv$$

$$Power = \frac{E}{t}$$

$$E = mg\Delta h$$

$$E = \frac{1}{2}mv^2$$

$$p = mv$$

$$Moment = Fd$$

$$Pressure = \frac{F}{A}$$

$$\rho_{density} = \frac{m}{V}$$

$$F = 6\pi\eta rv$$

Circular Motion & SHM:

$$F_c = \frac{mv^2}{r}$$

$$F = \frac{Gm_1m_2}{r^2}$$

$$\omega = \frac{\theta}{t} = \frac{v}{r} = 2\pi f$$

$$a = -\omega^2 x$$

$$x = A sin(\omega t + \theta)$$

$$v = \pm \omega \sqrt{A^2 - x^2}$$

$$T_{mass-spring} = 2\pi \sqrt{\frac{m}{k}}$$

$$T_{pendulum} = 2\pi \sqrt{\frac{l}{g}}$$

$$T_{u-pipe} = 2\pi \sqrt{\frac{l}{2g}}$$

Thermal Physics:

$$E = mc\Delta t$$

$$PV = nRT$$

Materials:

$$F = kx$$

$$E = \frac{1}{2}Fx$$

$$YM = \frac{stress}{strain} = \frac{F/A}{\Delta L/L}$$

$$K_{t-parallel} = K_1 + K_2$$

$$\frac{1}{K_{t-series}} = \frac{1}{K_1} + \frac{1}{K_2}$$

Electricity (C => Capacitance):

$$Q = It$$

$$W = QV$$

$$Voltage = IR = \frac{P}{I}$$

$$\epsilon = \frac{E}{Q} = I(R+r)$$

$$\frac{V_p}{V_s} = \frac{N_p}{N_s}$$

$$\rho = \frac{RA}{L}$$

$$E_{capacitor} = \frac{1}{2}CV^2$$

$$Q = CV$$

Particles:

$$E = mc^2$$

$$E = hf$$

$$eV = \frac{1}{2}mv_{max}^2$$

$$\frac{1}{2}mv_{max}^2 = hf - \phi$$

$$Debrogli \quad \lambda = \frac{h}{mv} = \frac{h}{p}$$

Waves:

$$c = f\lambda$$

$$T = \frac{1}{f}$$

$$n\lambda = d sin\theta$$

$$\lambda = \frac{dx}{L}$$

$$n_1 sin\theta_1 = n_2 sin\theta_2$$

$$f_1 = \frac{1}{2l}\sqrt{\frac{T}{\mu}}$$

Astro-physics:

$$T^2 \propto R^3$$

Chapter 3

Maths Formulae

Trigonometry:

Angle $\angle^s \rightarrow$ $\downarrow$ Value $\angle^s$	$0°$	$30°$	$45°$	$60°$	$90°$
$\sin\theta$	0	$\dfrac{1}{2}$	$\dfrac{1}{\sqrt{2}}$	$\dfrac{\sqrt{3}}{2}$	1
$\cos\theta$	1	$\dfrac{\sqrt{3}}{2}$	$\dfrac{1}{\sqrt{2}}$	$\dfrac{1}{2}$	0
$\tan\theta$	0	$\dfrac{1}{\sqrt{3}}$	1	$\sqrt{3}$	ND
$\csc\theta$	ND	2	$\sqrt{2}$	$\dfrac{2}{\sqrt{3}}$	1
$\sec\theta$	1	$\dfrac{2}{\sqrt{3}}$	$\sqrt{2}$	2	ND
$\cot\theta$	ND	$\sqrt{3}$	1	$\dfrac{1}{\sqrt{3}}$	0

$$\sin 2\theta = 2\sin\theta\cos\theta$$
$$\cos 2\theta = \cos^2\theta - \sin^2\theta$$

Pure maths:

$$f(x) = f(0) + f'(0)x + \frac{f''(0)}{2!}x^2 + \frac{f'''(0)}{3!}x^3...$$

$$(1+x)^n = 1 + nx + \frac{n(n-1)}{2!}x^2 + \frac{n(n-1)(n-2)}{3!}x^3...$$

$$x = \frac{-b \pm \sqrt{b^2 - 4ac}}{2a}$$

$${}^nC_r = \frac{n!}{r!(n-r)!}$$

Calculus:

$$\int uv' dx = uv - \int u'v dx$$

$$(f(g(x))' = g'(x)f'(g(x))$$

Arithemtic Sequences:

$$S_n = \frac{1}{2}n(a + l) = \frac{1}{2}n[2a + (n - 1)d]$$

Advanced Sequences:

$$S_n = \frac{a(1 - r^n)}{1 - r}$$

$$S_\infty = \frac{a}{1 - r}$$

$$\sum_{r=1}^{n} r = \frac{1}{2}n(n + 1)$$

$$\sum_{r=1}^{n} r^2 = \frac{1}{6}n(n + 1)(2n + 1)$$

$$\sum_{r=1}^{n} r^3 = \frac{1}{4}n^2(n + 1)^2$$

Chapter 4

Physics Notes

4.1 AS Particles and Radiation

4.1.1 Basics

- Inside the atom, electrons orbit the central nucleus in shells. The nucleus contains Z protons and A - Z neutrons.

$$_{Z:Protons}^{A:Mass}X$$

- Specific charge is the ratio of a particles charge to its mass, in coulombs per Kg.
- Isotopes have the same number of protons, but their nucleon number (mass => no. of neutrons) is different.

4.1.2 Stable and Unstable Nuclei

There are several different forces within a nucleus: gravitational, electromagnetic and the strong nuclear. The strong nuclear force is the only force which repels, in order to stop an atom/nucleus imploding in on itself. However, the strong nuclear force attracts within small distance (0 - 0.5fm) to stop the atom/nucleus exploding.

4.1.3 Decay

α decay: a helium nucleus is emitted, occurs if an atom is proton rich (>82).

$$_{Z}^{A}X \rightarrow_{Z-2}^{A-4} X +_{2}^{4} \alpha$$

β^- decay: an electron and an antineutrino are emitted, occurs if an atom is neutron rich. A neutron turns into a proton. The antineutrino carries away momentum.

$$_{Z}^{A}X \rightarrow_{Z+1}^{A} X +_{-1}^{0} \beta + \bar{\nu}_e$$

β^+ decay: a positron (positive electron) and a neutrino are emitted.

$$_{Z}^{A}X \rightarrow_{Z-1}^{A} X +_{+1}^{0} \beta + \nu_e$$

4.1.4 Photons

Photons are 'particles of light' and are known as discrete EM packets of quanta that carry energy. h(Planck's constant) $= 6.63 \times 10^{-34}$

$$E = hf = \frac{hc}{\lambda}$$

4.1.5 Antiparticles

- They have the same mass and rest energy, but a different charge. (neutrinos and antineutrinos have next to 0 rest energy as they are very small)

- Mass can be converted into energy. Energy can be converted to mass, when this occurs, both matter and anti-matter are created. This is known as 'pair production'.

$$E = mc^2$$

rest energy = total energy produced if mass $\rightarrow$ energy

min. energy needed for pair production = total rest energy of the produced particles

$$hf_{min} = E_{min} = 2E_0$$

- Annihilation = particle + anti-particle = 2 gamma ray photons. rest mass $\rightarrow$ rest energy. The 2 gamma ray photons conserve momentum.

$$E_{min} = E_0 = M_{min}c^2$$

4.1.6 Types of Particles

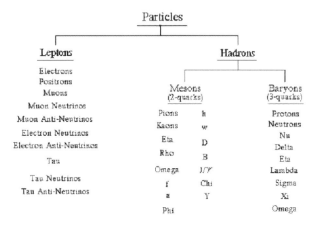

- All baryons (except protons) are unstable and eventually decay to a proton.
- Anti-baryons are the anti-particle of baryons.

- The total Baryon no. (B) never changes in an interaction.
- Mesons: B = 0.
- Leptons are fundamental particles and dont feel the strong nuclear force.

4.1.7 Particle Properties

Generation	Particle	Name	Lepton number	Mass $[m_e]$	Stability
e	e^-	electron	1	1	Yes
e	e^+	positron	-1	1	Yes
e	ν_e	electron-neutrino	1	~ 0	?
e	$\bar{\nu}_e$	anti-electron-neutrino	-1	~ 0	?
μ	μ^-	muon	1	~ 200	No
μ	μ^+	anti-muon	-1	~ 200	No
μ	ν_μ	muon-neutrino	1	~ 0	?
μ	$\bar{\nu}_\mu$	anti-muon-neutrino	-1	~ 0	?
τ	τ^-	tauon	1	~ 3500	No
τ	τ^+	anti-tauon	-1	~ 3500	No
τ	ν_μ	tau-neutrino	1	~ 0	?
τ	$\bar{\nu}_\tau$	anti-tau-neutrino	-1	~ 0	?

4.1.8 Strangeness

- Some particles have a quantum number called their strangeness.
- Strange particles are produced in pairs due to the conservation of strangeness.
- If the strangeness changes: weak interaction. If the strangeness remains the same: strong interaction.

4.1.9 Conservation of Properties

- Charge: conserved
- B no.: conserved
- L_μ no.: conserved
- L_e no.: conserved
- Strangeness: If it is not conserved $\rightarrow$ weak interaction

4.1.10 Quarks

Quark	symbol	charge	baryon number	strangeness
up	u	$+2/3\,e$	1/3	0
down	d	$-1/3\,e$	1/3	0
strange	s	$-1/3\,e$	1/3	-1

- Particles are made of quarks and antiquarks (anti-matter equivalent).
- Quark confinement: it is not possible to obtain a lone quark, if a quark is removed from a

particle a pair is produced similar to pair production.
- Neutrons (ddu) and protons (uud) have s = 0, $\therefore$ only U and D quarks are required.
- Baryons: 3 quarks
- Antibaryons: 3 antiquarks
- Meson quark composition:

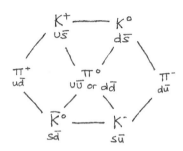

4.1.11   Particle Interactions

- All forces are created by exchange particles (virtual particles: exist for a short period to transfer energy).
- Exchange particles are also known as gauge bosons.
- Heavier exchange particles have a shorter range, as they require more energy and thus they exist for a shorter period of time.

Type	Exchange Particle	Particles affected
Strong	Pions (π^+, π^0, π^-)	Hadrons only
EM	Virtual Phton (γ)	Charged particles
Weak	W^+, W^- boson	All particles that contain quarks

4.1.12   Particle Interaction Diagrams

- Known as Feynman diagrams: exchange particles are wiggly' lines, other particles are represented by straight lines.
- Interactions can also be illustrated in terms of quarks.
- Rules:

1) Only for EM and weak interactions
2) Incoming particles start at the bottom.
3) Baryons stay on one side and Leptons stay on the other side.
4) W bosons carry charge from one side to the other, and charges MUST balance.
5) W^- going to the left = W^+ going to the right

β^+ Decay:

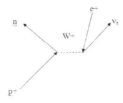

4.2 AS Quantum Phenomena

4.2.1 The Photoelectric Effect

- If light of a high enough frequency is shone on metal then it will instantly emit photo-electrons. The free electrons on or near the surface of the metal absorb energy from the radiation, breaking the atomic bonds if the energy is high enough.

- The axioms:

1) The frequency of the incident light (f_i) must be greater than the metal's threshold frequency (f_0).

$$f_i > f_0$$

2) The photoelectrons are emitted with a variety of kinetic energies, ranging from 0 to a maximum value.

$$E_{k_{max}} \quad \alpha \quad f_i$$

3) Intensity of radiation is the amount of energy per second hitting an area of the metal. $E_{k_{max}}$ is unaffected by the intensity of radiation.

4) number of photoelectons (n_p) is proportional to the intensity (I).

$$n_p \quad \alpha \quad I$$

- The threshold frequency (f_0) illustrates that no matter the intensity of the incoming photons or the time period over which it is measured, the photo electric effect will never occur unless the incident frequency of photons is greater than f_0. This is the photon model of light, if wave theory was used, then the photo electric effect would occur given enough time, no matter the incident photon frequency.

- The higher the intensity of the incident photons, the more energy should be transferred to the electrons in the metal and thus $E_{K_{max}}$ should be higher. However this is not the case as $E_{K_{max}}$ depends on the frequency of the incident photons.

4.2.2 Photon Model of Light

- Photons are 'particles of light' known as discrete packets of quanta. All the energy of one photon transfers to one single electron. The energy of a photon is determined by its frequency:

$$E = hf = \frac{hc}{\lambda}$$

- The energy of the electrons must be greater than the work function of the metal (ϕ). The threhold frequency (f_0) is the minimum frequency of the incident photons in order for electrons to be emitted:

$$hf_0 = \phi \rightarrow f_0 = \frac{\phi}{h}$$

4.2.3 Kinetic Energy

- The kinetic energy of the photoelectrons come as a range of energies and thus only $E_{k_{max}}$ can be considered:

$$hf = \phi + E_{k_{max}} = \phi + \frac{1}{2}mv_{max}^2$$

4.2.4 Stopping Potential

- The stopping potential is the voltage (V_s) required to stop the fastest moving electron ($e = 1.6 \times 10^{-19}$):

$$eV_s = E_{k_{max}}$$

4.2.5 Measuring Planck's Constant

4.2.6 Energy Levels

- The electron volt (eV) is the kinetic energy carried by an electron after it has been accelerated through a potential difference of 1 volt.

- Electrons can only exist in certain well-defined energy levels (i.e. shells). Where $n = 1$ is the lowest energy level, known as the ground state. n=∞ is when there is zero energy, which implies that as you go down the energy levels, the energy gets lower (i.e. more negative).

- Electron transition: electron moves down an energy level, emitting a photon as energy.

- Electron excitation: electron moves up an energy level by absorbing a photon:

$$\Delta E = E_1 - E_2 = hf$$

- When an electron is removed from an atom, the atom is ionised and now has a charge.

4.2.7   Photon Emission and Line Spectra

- Photon emission: voltage across mercury gas, accelerating the electrons, and ionising the atoms, producing even more electrons. These electrons excite the electrons in the mercury atoms, and thus as result they produce photons as UV light. A phosphorus coating on the inside of the tube absorbs the photons, exciting the electrons and making them rise up the energy levels. They then cascade back down the energy levels emitting photons from the visible light spectrum.

- Line emission: exciting particles fall down the energy levels emitting photons of a certain energy level, thus only those lines appear.

- Line absorption: white light passes through a cool gas, the gas's electrons absorb certain energy photons, resulting in a spectrum where certain colours cannot be seen.

- Energy of an ecccelerated electron:

$$eV = E_k = \frac{1}{2}mv^2$$

4.2.8   Wave-Particle Duality

- Diffraction infers that light acts as a wave, as only interference can occur with waves. However the photoelectric effect shows have light also acts as particles.

- The De Broglie wavelength relates a wave property to a moving particle:

$$\lambda = \frac{h}{mv}$$

4.2.9   Electron Diffraction

- Electrons have a smaller De Broglie wavelength and thus do not diffract that much as their mass is larger than photons.

4.3 AS Waves

4.3.1 The EM spectrum

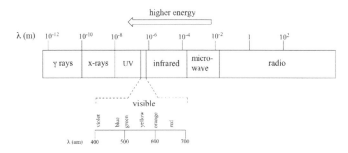

4.3.2 Progressive Wave Basics

- Propagates through a material without transferring any energy to the material, yet carrying energy e.g. a buoy in the sea does not move laterally, only vertically.
- Waves can be reflected, refracted and diffracted.

Terms:
- Phase: a measurement of the position of a certain point along the wave cycle.
- Phase difference: the amount by which one wave lags behind another.
- Period: time for 1 oscillation.
- Frequency: number of oscillations in 1 second.

$$f = \frac{1}{T}$$
$$c = f\lambda$$

- Wave speed can be measured with 2 microphones a known distance apart.

4.3.3 Types

- Transverse: displacement of the particles is perpendicular to the direction of propagation (e.g. EM). Peaks and troughs indicate points of max and min amplitude.
- Longitudinal: displacement of the particles is parallel to the direction of propagation (e.g. sound). Rarefractions and compressions indicate points of max and min amplitude.

- Polarisation: blocks out transverse movement in a certain plane (note: longitudinal waves cannot be polarised). e.g. light reflected off snow is partially polarised, TV signals are polarised in the direction of the transmitter antenna.

4.3.4 Superposition and Interference

- Superposition: when do or more waves of similar type, the resultant displacement is the vecotr sum of the individual displacements. Constructive: displacements add. Destructive:

displacements partially/fully cancel.
- To calculate phase difference, simply note the difference in position (in radians) between to points, one on each curve.

4.3.5   Stationary Waves

- The superposition of two progressive waves of the same frequency and amplitude, moving in opposite directions, resulting in a stationary wave which transmits no energy.
- Displacement node: position of maximum displacement (pressure anti-node).
- Displacement anti-node: position of minimum displacement (pressure node).

- Resonant frequencies occur when $\frac{k\lambda}{2}$ can fit across the entire stationary wave's span. i.e. the first harmonic (fundamental frequency) is when half a wave length can fit into the wave's span.

- An example of this can be observed with a speaker in a closed tube that has sand in, the sand will form around the displacement nodes - areas of the least displacement (i.e. pressure anti-nodes - areas of low pressure).
- The resonant frequency can be calculated by:

$$f_1 = \frac{1}{2L}\sqrt{\frac{T}{\mu}}$$

$$f_n = \frac{n}{2L}\sqrt{\frac{T}{\mu}}$$

4.3.6   Diffraction

- When a progressive wave 'bends', explained by Huygens wave model.
- Let $gap = d$ and $wave - length = \lambda$:
$d > \lambda$: (many times larger) diffraction is unnoticeable.
$d > \lambda$: (several times larger) diffraction is noticeable.
$d = \lambda$: maximum possible diffraction.
$d < \lambda$: waves are mostly reflected back.

- Waves can also diffract around objects, where a shadow forms, but then the waves meet up again.

- When light shines through a single slit, an interference pattern occurs, with a central bright maxima and alternating fringes of constructive and destructive interference. This pattern occurs as a result of the light diffracting, to understand why points on a wave may arrive in phase and may arrive out of phase, again, Huygens wave front theory has to be considered.

- The light source must be coherent and monochromatic (e.g. a laser). White light would result in a spectra appearing, with only the central maxima being white.

- Intensity: power per unit area:
1) Increasing the slit width, decreases diffraction but increases the intensity of the maxima.
2) Increasing the wavelength of the light, increases diffraction but decreases the intensity of the maxima.

4.3.7 Two Source Interference

- When two coherent and monochromatic wave sources meet:

1) In phase: constructive interference. Occurs when the path difference (amount by which the path travelled by one wave is longer than the path travelled by the other wave) is:

$$n\lambda$$

2) Out of Phase: destructive interference. Occurs when the path difference is:

$$(n + \frac{1}{2})\lambda$$

4.3.8 Young's Double Slit

- Passing a coherent and monochromatic light source through a double slit causes the light to diffract and then interfere. This forms a pattern of maxima and minima lines, determined by the equation:

$$w(fringe - spacing) = \frac{\lambda D(slit - screen - distance)}{s(slit - seperation)}$$

- The assumption that $\sin \theta = \theta$ for small angles has to be used.
- This experiment is evidence that light exists as a wave.

4.3.9 Diffraction Gratings

- A filter with many slits, separated by d metres.
- Produces an interference pattern of dots as opposed to lines. The dots are equally spaced, labelled as the nth dot. The 0th order line is the central one.
- The equation is:
$$d \sin \theta = n\lambda$$

4.3.10 The Refractive Index

- Light refracts (speed and wavelength decrease, frequency remains constant) towards the normal when it passes to a more optically dense material. The optical density of materials can be compared via the refractive index:

$$n = \frac{C}{C_s}$$

- The relative refractive index going from material 1 to material 2:

$$_1n_2 = \frac{C_1}{C_2} = \frac{n_2}{n_1}$$

- Snell's Law:

$$n_1 \sin \theta_1 = n_2 \sin \theta_2$$

4.3.11 Total Internal Reflection

- A phenomenon whereby light which passes to a more optically dense material reflects. This occurs when the angle of incidence is greater than the critical angle of that material (θ_c).

$$\sin \theta_c = \frac{n_2}{n_1}$$

- Even if the angle of incidence is less than the critical angle, partial reflection still occurs.

- Optical fibres are thin with a less optically dense cladding relative to the core, to ensure TIR occurs.

- Absorption: loss of signal amplitude due to the material absorbed the signal.
- Modal Dispersion (broadens the signal): light takes different (i.e. shorter or longer) paths down the fibre, meaning the light can arrive at different times (solution: narrow fibre).
- Material Dispersion (broadens the signal): light consists of many different wavelengths, which will diffract by different amounts in a material (solution: monochromatic source).

4.4   AS Mechanics

4.4.1   Scalars and Vectors

- A scalar quantity only has magnitude, for example speed.
- A vector quantity has magnitude and direction, for example velocity.

- scalar $\times$ vector = vector
- scalar $\times$ scalar = scalar
- vector $\times$ vector = scalar

4.4.2   Moments

- A moment is the 'size of a force times the perpendicular distance between the line of action of the force and the turning point'.

$$M = F \times d$$

- A couple is a pair of forces of equal size which act parallel to each other but in opposite directions.
- An object will topple if the line of action of its weight is past the pivot point of the object.

4.4.3   Newton's Laws of Motion

1st : The conservation of energy law, if a resultant force does not act on a body, it will continue with its current velocity.

2nd : $F = \frac{d}{dt}mv$

3rd : If body A exerts a force on body B, then body B exerts an equal, but opposite force on body A.

- Terminal speed is when: $weight = drag$, drag is determined by (k is a constant, and C_d is the unitless drag constant):

$$F_d = kv^2 = \frac{1}{2}C_D A\rho v^2$$

4.4.4 Displacement, Velocity and Acceleration

$$S \to V \to A$$

$$V = \frac{d}{dt}S \quad A = \frac{d}{dt}V$$

$$V = \int A\,dt \quad S = \int V\,dt$$

This also means that the gradient of a s/t graph is velocity at that instant, gradient of a v/t grah is acceleration at that instant, area under an a/t graph is change in velocity and finally, area under a v/t graph is displacement.

4.4.5 Projectiles

- Horizontal: acceleration is $0ms^{-1}$ if air resistance is ignored, thus velocity remains constant.
- Vertical: acceleration is due to gravity (i.e. g), and thus follows a parabolic motion in the vertical plane (vertical displacement against time), as well a s a parabola in 2 planes.

4.4.6 Momentum

$$P = M \times \nu$$

Momentum is **always** conserved, kinetic energy is not always conserved.

Collision Type	Momentum	Kinetic Energy
Elastic	Conserved	Conserved
Inelastic	Conserved	Not conserved
Explosive - e.g. alpha decay	-	-

Determines whether a collision is elastic or inelastic by comparing the velocities of the relevant objects. For a one-dimensional collision, if an elastic collision occurs the coefficient $= 1$, if an inelastic collision occurs the coefficient $= 0$. It is given by:

$$C_r = e = \frac{\nu_2 - \nu_1}{u_1 - u_2}$$

- An impulse is the the change in time times force which is equal to the change in linear momentum and illustrates how increasing the time, will decrease the force acting on an object in order to maintain the value of linear momentum.

$$F\Delta t = \Delta p$$

4.4.7 Centre of Mass

$$x_m = \frac{\sum_{r=1}^{n} m_r x_r}{\sum_{r=1}^{n} m_r}$$

4.4.8   Energy and Power

$$GPE = mg\Delta h$$
$$E_k = \frac{1}{2}mv^2$$
$$workdone = W = distance \times force = Fd$$
$$P = Fv$$

- Remember: force is a vector so work done is also a vector since it is in the direction of motion.

- If the force is acting at an angle θ to the direction of motion, then the work done is a component of Fd/Fv.

- If potential energy is completely converted into kinetic energy.

$$v = \sqrt{2g\Delta h}$$

- Efficiency (DC electric motor):

$$efficiency = \frac{useful}{total} = \frac{mg\Delta h}{VIt}$$

4.4.9   Mechanical Ratios

- Compares how the effective force can be 'increased' in certain mechanical systems e.g. teeth in gears: a cog with more teeth can make a cog with less teeth turn quicker as a single revolution results in a larger distance travelled.

- Just consider the ratio between the common aspect (turns of input:turns of output):
1) Gear teeth:driven teeth.
2) Smaller diameter pulley:larger diameter pulley.
3) Pulleys: number of original 'tensions'compared with number of new 'tensions'

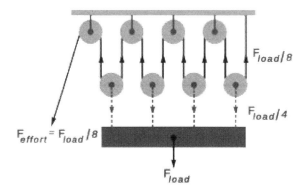

4.5 AS Electricity

4.5.1 Terms

- Current: rate of flow of electrons (charge).
- Charge: the magnitude of electrical polarity in a circuit (1 Coulomb: amount of charge that passes in 1 second when the current is 1 ampere).
- Potential difference: the work done in moving a unit of charge between two points.
- Resistance: the ratio of potential difference between two points to the curret that flows between those two points.
- Ohm's law: current is $\propto$ potential difference.
- Internal resistance: the resistance inside of a cell due to the presence of ions.
- e.m.f. (electromotive force): lost volts + terminal potential difference (the energy transferred when 1 unit of charge flows through the load resistance).

4.5.2 Components

- Thermistor: high resistance at low temperatures, low resistance at high temperatures.
- LDR: high resistance at low light levels, low resistance at high light levels.
- Superconductor: have no resistance below a certain transitional temperature,
- Semiconductor: conducts under certain conditions - there is a breakdown voltage after which the semiconductor conducts.

4.5.3 equations

$$I = \frac{\Delta Q}{\Delta t}$$
$$W = QV$$
$$V = IR$$
$$P = VI$$
$$E = Pt = VIt$$
$$\rho = \frac{RA}{L}$$
$$\epsilon = \frac{E}{Q}$$
$$\epsilon = I(R + r)$$

4.5.4 Non-Ohmic Conductors

- As the current increases, the component's resistance increases. Thus Ohm's law does not apply.
- Diodes have a sudden voltage drop (i.e. threshold voltage ≈ 0.6v), they also allow (little) current in the reverse direction.

4.5.5 Kirchhoff's Laws

1) Total current entering a junction = total current leaving a junction
2) The total e.m.f. around a series circuit = the sum of the p.d.s across each component

4.5.6 Resistor Networks

- Series:
$$R_T = R_1 + R_2...$$

- Parallel:
$$R_T = \frac{R_1 R_2 R_3...}{R_1 + R_2 + R_3...}$$

- Current always flows from an area of high potential to an area of low potential. Thus if the potential at two points is the same, there will be no current.
- The Wheatstone bridge is a good example of this:

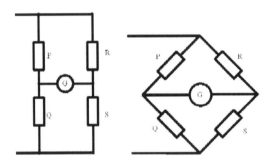

$$if \quad \frac{P}{R} = \frac{Q}{R} => G = 0 amps$$

- The current at G is 0A because: The potential at each junction is the same, thus there is no difference in potential and current cannot flow (Kirchhoff's 1st Law has to also be preserved so the sum of the currents at each junction has to be the same).

4.5.7 Power Loss in Cables

- First use $P = VI$ to calculate the current.
- Then use $P = I^2 R$ to calculate the power loss.

- e.g.
Power transmitted = $1GW$ at $400kV$ => $I = \frac{P}{V} = \frac{1 \times 10^9}{4 \times 10^5} = 2500A$
Resistance of cables = 5Ω => Power loss = $I^2 R = 2500^2 \times 5 = 31MW$

4.5.8 Transfomers

- Transformer work in ratios between the voltage across the primary coil and voltage across the secondary coil:

$$\frac{V_1}{coil_1} = \frac{V_2}{coil_2}$$

- More turns on the secondary coil ($coil_2$) results in a higher voltage across the secondary coil BUT a lower current since power is conserved (neglecting any inefficiencies).

4.6   AS Materials

4.6.1   Density

- Ratio of a material's mass to it's volume.

$$\rho = \frac{m}{V}$$

4.6.2   Hooke's Law

- The force applied to a material is directly proportional to the extension of the material as a result of that force.

$$F = k\Delta x$$

- This law works for both compressive and tensile forces.

- Limit of Proportionality: the point at which the extension is no longer proportional to the force.
- Elastic limit: just past the LoP, beyond this point the material deforms plastically (atoms are permanently deformed) and does not return to its original shape.

- An elastic stretch occurs when a material, such as an elastic band, is stretched, and Hooke's Law no longer applies.

4.6.3   Stress and Strain

$$stress = \frac{force}{area}$$
$$strain = \frac{\Delta length}{length}$$

- Breaking stress: the stress that is large enough to break the material.
- Ultimate Tensile Stress: max stress a material can withstand.
- Yield Point: point at which the material begins to extend without any further load.

- If the extension is elastic: elastic strain energy is converted into kinetic energy.
- If the extension is plastic: elastic strain energy is also converted into heat energy.

4.6.4   Young's Modulus

$$YM = E = \frac{stress}{strain} = \frac{F/A}{\Delta L/L} = \frac{FL}{A\Delta L}$$

4.6.5   Graphs

- Area under a stress/strain graph is the 'strain energy per unit volume'.

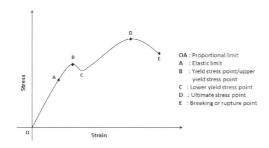

- The area under a F/x graph is the elastic strain energy. Also known as the work done.

$$E = \frac{1}{2}kx^2$$

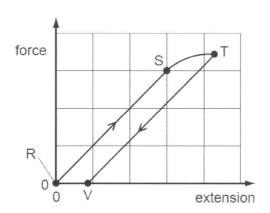

4.6.6   Brittle Materials

- A brittle material has a sudden breaking point and does not deform plastically.
- Brittle materials marginally elastically deform before a 'brittle fracture' occurs.
- The atoms are crystallised within the atomic structure.

4.7   A2 Astro-Physics

4.7.1   Kepler's Laws

1) The Law of Orbits: All planets move in elliptical orbits, with the sun at one focus.

2) The Law of Areas: A line that connects a planet to the sun sweeps out equal areas in equal times.

3) The Law of Periods: $T^2 \propto R^3$

4.7.2   Structure of the Solar System

- Order of the planets: McVEMJSUNP

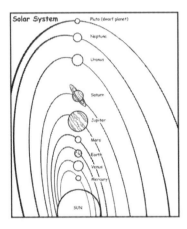

4.7.3   Phases of the Moon

- Annular eclipse: occurs when the Moon covers the Sun's center, leaving the Sun's visible outer edges.

4.7.4   Comets and Asteroids

- Comet: a small rocky body orbiting the sun.
- Asteroid: a body that orbits the sun consisting of a nucleus of ice and dust and, when near the sun, a 'tail' of gas and dust particles always pointing away from the sun.

4.8 A2 Further Mechanics

4.8.1 Circular Motion

- Radians is another measure of angles, conversion: $180^o = \pi^c$
- Angular speed (ω) is the change in angle over time. ω: angular speed in $rads^{-1}$

$$\omega = \frac{\theta}{t} = \frac{v}{r}$$

- If the time is one period (T) of rotation; $\theta = 2\pi$ and t=T.

$$\omega = 2\pi f$$

4.8.2 Centripetal Force and Acceleration

- Objects that travel in a circle have a constant speed v. If you were to resolve the forces, the velocity always increases as the direction is always changing. This results in an acceleration towards the centre of the circle. $F = ma$, which implies that there must be a force acting towards the centre of the circle i.e. centripetal force. There must be a force acting inwards on an object travelling in a circle in order for it not to simply just travel in a straight line.

$$a = \frac{v^2}{r} = \omega^2 r$$

$$F_c = ma = \frac{mv^2}{r} = m\omega^2 r$$

- Centripetal force is the resultant force at any one point. For example, the centripetal force of a car going around a bend is provided by the friction of the road on the tyres, as this is the only horizontal force.

$$F_r = F_c$$

4.8.3 SHM

- Simple Harmonic Motion can be described as: an oscillation in which the acceleration of an object is directly proportional to its displacement (x) from its equilibrium position, and is directed towards the equilibrium position. These two conditions are necessary for a system to demonstrate SHM.

$$a = -kx = -\omega^2 x$$

- When the displacement from the equilibrium position is equal to the amplitude, the acceleration is the greatest but the velocity is 0.
- The period (generally) remains the same as the period of oscillation is independent of amplitude (known as isochronous).

- Derivation of formulae requires you to understand that SHOs and the graphs of SHM can be compared to a circle. y is the vertical displacement, as t is along the x-axis. Resolving vertically, gives the displacement as $y = r \sin \theta$, where r is the circle's radius and is thus the amplitude (A). ($+ \theta$ provides the phase shift)

$$\omega = \frac{\theta}{t}$$

$$\theta = \omega t = 2\pi f t$$

$$y = A \sin(2\pi f t + \theta)$$

- Differentiating can derive the velocity and acceleration formulae, which can be solved to obtain:

$$a = -ky = -\omega^2 y$$

$$\therefore k = \omega^2$$

$$v = \pm \omega \sqrt{A^2 - y^2}$$

4.8.4   SHM Mass-Spring System

- Spring must not deform plastically and must be open coil.
- Overall spring constant alters in the opposite manner to resistors i.e. parallel: add spring constants, series: spring constant decreases.
- Weight (mg) can be ignored as it is cancelled out by the initial extension of the spring.
- Remember: period is independent of amplitude.
- y is the displacement as the system is being looked at vertically.

$$F = -ky = ma$$

$$a = -\frac{k}{m}y$$

$$\omega^2 = \frac{k}{m}$$

$$\omega = \frac{2\pi}{T} = \sqrt{\frac{k}{m}}$$

$$\therefore T = 2\pi \sqrt{\frac{m}{k}}$$

4.8.5   SHM Pendulum System

- Air resistance does not affect the period but it does decrease the max amplitude.
- The angle must be small in order for: $\theta = \sin \theta$
- x is now the displacement, as the system is being looked at horizontally.

$$F = -mg \sin \theta = -mg\theta = ma$$

$$a = -g\theta = -\frac{g}{l}x$$

$$\omega^2 = \frac{g}{l}$$

$$\omega = \frac{2\pi}{T} = \sqrt{\frac{g}{l}}$$

$$\therefore T = 2\pi\sqrt{\frac{l}{g}}$$

4.8.6 SHM Water in a U-Pipe

- The equation for time period can be derived by comparing the potential and the kinetic energy of the water in the pipe as well as resolving the forces involved.

$$T = 2\pi\sqrt{\frac{l}{2g}}$$

4.8.7 SHM Energy

- Potential and kinetic energy are complete opposites in the respect that when kinetic energy is at a maximum, potential energy is usually at a minimum.

$$E_k = \frac{1}{2}mv^2 = \frac{1}{2}m(A\omega \cos{(\omega t)})^2 = \frac{1}{2}mA^2\omega^2 \cos^2{(\omega t)}$$

- Thus E_k is always positive, and is a *cos* squared curve.
- E_p would be a *sin* squared curve.
- E_T would be the sum of the energies at any moment in time, and is always equivalent to the max amplitude.

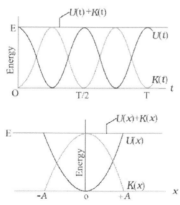

4.8.8 Damping

- A decrease in the amplitude of an SHM oscillator due to a loss of energy as a result of frictional/resistive forces. The period is NOT affected, only the amplitude is affected. Damping results in an exponential decrease in amplitude.

- Systems are often deliberately dampened either to reduce the effects of resonance or to reduce the amplitude to 0 as quickly as possible (e.g. car suspension).

- Types:
1) Light damping: Amplitude only reduces a small amount over every period.
2) Heavy damping: Amplitude noticably reduces over every period.
3) Critical damping: Amplitude returns to zero before a period is completed. The quickest method of reducing SHO.
4) Overdamping: Greater damping than critical damping but takes a long time (e.g. a soft close door).

- Resonance peaks as a result of damping:

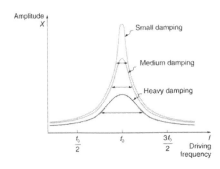

4.8.9 Free and Forced Vibrations

- Free vibration: the oscillator experiences no increase/decrease in energy from the surroundings. Oscillations occur at the system's natural frequency.
- Forced vibration: a driving oscillator also vibrates an SHM oscillator, changing the frequency in some way.

- In Phase: $f_d < f_n$.
- Out of Phase (by π): $f_d > f_n$ (oscillator won't be able to keep up with the driving frequency).
- $f_d = f_n$, resonance occurs and the phase difference is exactly $\frac{\pi}{2}$. As the driving frequency approaches the natural frequency, the amplitude of the orginal oscillator gradually increases.

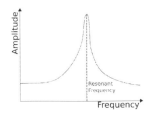

- Uses for resonance: to break kidney stones, musical instruments.
- When resonance is unwanted: on bridges.

4.9   A2 Fields

4.9.1   Centre of Gravity

- The centre of gravity depends on the strength of the gravitational field, i.e. as you go up Mount Everest, the gravitational field strength decreases resulting in an overall centre of gravity that is lower than the centre of mass.

4.9.2   Gravitational Fields

- A force field is a region in which a body experiences a non-contact force.
- Gravitational fields are radial, where the arrows are directed towards the larger mass (usually a planet).
- $F \propto \frac{1}{r^2}$, thus the gravitational field strength decreases with distance:

$$F = \frac{Gm_1 m_2}{r^2}$$

- Gravitational field strength is the force per unit mass (gravitational field strength is the same as the same value as the acceleration due to gravity value):

$$g = \frac{F}{m}$$

- The force due to a gravitational field is as a result of a body's weight:

$$F = m_1 g = \frac{Gm_1 m_2}{r^2}$$

$$g = \frac{Gm_2}{r^2}$$

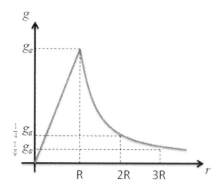

- If there are two objects (e.g. planets) with fields, there will be a neutral point where the forces cancel out.

4.9.3 Gravitational Potential (V)

- The gravitational potential energy a unit mass has at a specific point.

$$V = -\frac{Gm_2}{r}$$

- A mass at infinite distance has zero gravitational potential, as result as you get closer to the planet it decreases and thus you get 'negative' gravitational potential.

$$g = -\frac{\Delta V}{\Delta r}$$

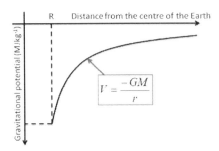

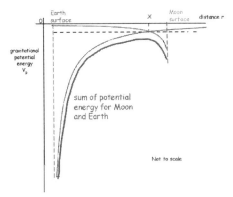

- Planet of mass M, radius R and distance from the centre at any given point r. Thus the equation applies to this scenario, however in order to calculate escape velocity kinetic energy has to be calculated, using the equation:

$$w = fd \therefore$$

$$energy_{total} = \sum_{r=R}^{\infty} fr$$

Thus the area under the graph is equal to the total work done.

$$\int_R^\infty \frac{GMm}{r^2}dr = \left[-\frac{GMm}{r}\right]_R^\infty = (0) - \left(-\frac{GMm}{R}\right) = \frac{GMm}{R}$$

This is now the total energy required to escape the gravitational field, which is up until the point when GPE is equal to zero, and thus only kinetic energy remains:

$$\frac{GMm}{R} = \frac{1}{2}m\nu^2$$

$$\therefore \nu = \sqrt{\frac{2GM}{R}}$$

4.9.4 Gravitational Potential Difference

- It is the energy needed to move a unit mass.

$$WD = \Delta W = m\Delta V$$

- An equipotential surface is perpendicular to the field, and thus moving along it require no work in the direction of the field.

4.9.5 Orbits

- To calculate all the formulae for orbits, equate the force equation for gravitational fields to the centripetal force equation.
- To calculate the escape velocity equate work done and kinetic energy.

- Geostationary orbit: a geosynchronous orbit but also fixed relative to a point at the surface of the Earth and has an orbital path along the equator.
- Geosynchronous orbit: orbital period = rotational period of the Earth.
- Low Earth Orbits: orbit at a time period much shorter than that of the earth's rotational period in order to overcome the increased gravitational field strength.

4.9.6 Electric Fields

- They can either be attractive or repulsive, depending on the charge of the point charges. They only enact on charged bodies (i.e. any body that is charged has an electric field).
- Opposite charges attract, similar charges repel.
- Coulomb's law (ε_0: permittivity of free space):

$$F \propto \frac{1}{r^2}$$

$$F = \frac{1}{4\pi\varepsilon_0}\frac{Q_1Q_2}{r^2} \approx \frac{9 \times 10^9 \times Q_1Q_2}{r^2}$$

- Electric field strength (NC^{-1}): the force per unit positive charge.

$$E = \frac{F}{Q} = \frac{\Delta V}{r} = \frac{Voltage}{r}$$

- Where Q is the charge of the of the object.

4.9.7 Types of Electric Fields

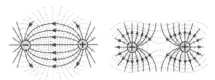

- Plate charges: lines are parallel for the opposite charges, but skew away for similar charges.
- Conducting paper and electrolytic tanks can be used to illustrate field lines.

4.9.8 (Absolute) Electric Potential

- The electric potential energy that a unit positive charge would have at a certain point OR The work done in moving a unit charge between two points. Represented by V and measured in volts.

$$\Delta W = Q\Delta V = Fd$$

- This can also be recalled from the equation:

$$eV = \frac{1}{2}mv^2$$

- For a positive force (repulsive force), the graph is above the x-axis.
- For a negative charge (attractive force), the graph is below the x-axis.

4.9.9 Gravitational vs. Electric Fields

Similarities: Both have inverse-square force laws that have many characteristics in common, eg use of field lines, use of potential concept, equipotential surfaces etc

Differences: masses always attract, but charges may attract or repel.

4.10   A2 Fluid Dynamics (in detail)

4.10.1   Basic Equations

$$density = \frac{mass}{volume}$$

$$pressure = \frac{force}{area}$$

4.10.2   Fluid Pressure

Take a cylindrical column of liquid, of height h and cross-sectional area A. The volume of the column is Ah, the mass of the column is ρAh ($\because mass = density \times volume$), the weight is ρAhg and finally

$$pressure \quad on \quad A = \frac{\rho Ahg}{A} = \rho hg$$

The upthrust, or buoyancy is the same as the resultant force on the column which is equal to the difference between the force on the top surface and the force on the bottom surface. An object will float if it is less dense than the fluid surrounding it, i.e. upthrust > weight.

$$\therefore Air \quad pressure = \rho \Delta hg$$

Δh is the difference in height between the edge of the atmosphere and the height of measurement, from the Earth's surface. Thus as altitude increases, Δh decreases. Atmospheric pressure decreases exponentially, this can be proved with the equation above and the ideal gas equation.

4.10.3   Viscosity and Turbulence

Viscosity is the internal resistance of the molecules in a liquid which causes a resistance to flow. Viscosity is defined as the rate of shear stress of the fluid per velocity gradient.

Low viscosity = turn turbulent from laminar at low velocities.
High viscosity = remains laminar even at higher velocities.

Reynolds number determines the flow, if it is below 1000, the flow will remain laminar.

$$R = \frac{\nu r \rho}{\eta}$$

R is Reynold's number, ν is the fluid flow velocity, r is a certain dimension (e.g. radius of a tube), ρ is the density of the fluid and η is the viscosity.

Kinematic Viscosity:

$$\frac{\eta}{\rho}$$

If the ratio of viscosity to density is higher, the fluid will remain laminar at higher velocities.

4.10.4 Bernoulli's Equation

Often in fluid dynamics fluid friction has to be ignored (i.e. viscosity) and the assumption that the fluid is incompressible and has a laminar flow has to made. The equation of continuity compares the flow velocity of a fluid from a larger cross-sectional area gradually moving into a small cross-sectional area.

$$\frac{\nu_2}{\nu_1} = \frac{A_1}{A_2}$$

This concept is built upon with Bernoulli's equation:

$$p + \frac{1}{2}\rho\nu^2 + \rho gh$$

This results in a constant.

p is the surrounding air pressure. ρgh accounts for the effect of gravity if the flow is not equipotential (has a vertical component), and is known as static pressure (potential energy per unit volume). $\frac{1}{2}\rho\nu^2$ is dynamic pressure (kinetic pressure per unit volume), both combined is equal to total pressure. The equation illustrates the conservation of energy per unit volume.

Dynamic pressure and static pressure can be equated to solve problems. For example, static pressure would occur at the top of a reservoir, dynamic pressure would occur at the outlet for the water.

According to Bernoulli's equation, if the fluid velocity increases, it results in a decrease in vertical pressure (in order to keep the pressure total pressure constant), however the lateral pressure increases.

4.10.5 Aerodynamics

There are four forces that act on a plane: lift, weight, thrust and fluid friction (drag). Planes will stall when the flow over the aerofoil turns turbulent and fails to be laminar, curved wings greatly increase the ratio of lift to drag and provide a small streamline (i.e. decreased drag).

Lift occurs due to the air on the top of the aerofoil having a greater flow velocity than the air below it. Using Bernoulli's equation, this results in a lower pressure at the top and a higher pressure below. The air flows slower below the aerofoil due to the area in which it is able to flow being restricted, whereas the exact opposite occurs above. This can be compared to a pipe:

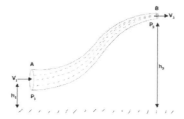

4.10.6 Magnus effect

Utilises the design of a special wing to create lift (in any direction), has greater lift but also greater drag and thus a lower lift to drag ratio. The spinning column results in air being dragged round the other side of the column resulting in the fluid flow velocity being relatively higher on one side compared to the other, this results in a pressure difference, generating thrust. The Flettner Rotor Ship uses the Magnus effect.

4.10.7 Pressure differential and the Venturi effect

A Venturi meter measures the pressure differential between two points, which can be used to calculate the fluid velocity.

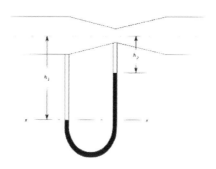

4.11 A2 Capacitors

4.11.1 Basics

- The capacitance of an object is the amount of charge it is able to store per unit potential difference across it.
- A capacitor is similar to a cell, however it discharges and charges very quickly, and does not dtore as much charge.
- A capacitor is made up of two electrical conducting plates separated by an insulator (a dielectric).
- Recall:

$$I = \frac{Q}{t}$$

- Capcitance equation:

$$Q = CV$$

4.11.2 Energy

$$E = \frac{1}{2}QV = \frac{1}{2}CV^2$$

4.11.3 Charging and Discharging

- Charging:
1) As time progresses, current decreases, but the rate of current decrease decreases (i.e. an asymptote).
2) As time progresses, the potential difference across the capacitor increases, but the rate of potential difference increase decreases (i.e. an asymptote).
3) As time progresses, charge increases, but the rate of charge increase decreases (i.e. an asymptote).

- Discharging:
1) As time progresses, current decreases, but the rate of current decrease decreases (i.e. an asymptote).
2) As time progresses, the potential difference across the capacitor decreases, but the rate of potential difference decrease decreases (i.e. an asymptote).
3) As time progresses, charge decreases, but the rate of charge decrease decreases (i.e. an asymptote).

4.11.4 Time Constant

- The time taken for a capacitor to charge to 63% or discharge to 37% (time constant) is denoted by τ. (R is the total resistance of the circuit).

$$\tau = RC$$

- In theory the total time to charge/discharge $= 5\tau = 5RC$.
- The time taken for the potential difference, current or charge to half is goven by the half life:

$$t_{\frac{1}{2}} = 0.69RC$$

Chapter 5

Maths Notes

5.1 Graph Sketching

5.1.1 Common Functions

5.1.2 Drawing Unseen Functions

- Steps to find general shape:

1) Roots (i.e. when $x = 0$ and when $y = 0$)
2) Max/Min pts.
3) Vertical asymptotes
4) Values as $x \to \infty$, $x \to -\infty$, $x \to$ (i.e. horizontal asymptotes)
5) Values as $y \to \infty$, $y \to -\infty$. May need to refer to 3)
6) Try common values and points if extra information is required.

5.1.3 Example

- Draw the function:

$$f(x) = \frac{4 - x}{x^2 + 3x + 2}$$

1) When $f(x) = 0 = 4 - x$, thus the only x-axis root is when $x = 4$. When $x = 0$, $f(x) = 2$.
2) $f'(x) = \frac{x^2 - 8x - 14}{(x^2 + 3x + 2)^2}$, thus when $f'(x) = 0$, $x^2 - 8x - 14 = 0$. This means that the stationary points occur when: $x = 4 + \sqrt{30}, x = 4 - \sqrt{30}$.
3) The only undefined values occur when $x^2 + 3x + 2 = 0 \to (x + 2)(x + 1) = 0$, thus the asymptotes (x) are $x = -2$ and $x = -1$.
4) Divided every term in the fraction by the highest order x term on the denominator, giving:

$$f(x) = \frac{\frac{4}{x^2} - \frac{1}{x}}{1 + \frac{3}{x} + \frac{2}{x^2}}$$

The only value x cannot take in the new format of $f(x)$ is 0. However we have already found that $f(x)$ can $= 0$. Thus, the only horizontal asymptote occurs when $x \to \infty$ (PTO).
$x \to \infty => f(x) \to 0$ This is an asymptote, the only one in the horizontal direction.

5) See 3)

6) Extra information not needed

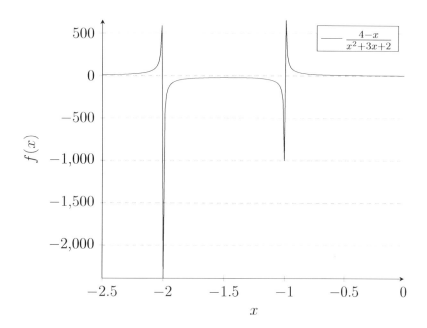

5.1.4 Other Methods

- Another effective method is to consider a function as the multiple of two other known functions:

$$f(x) = \frac{\sin x}{x} = (\frac{1}{x})(\sin x)$$

Thus,

$$f(x)$$

will take the shape of a $y = sinx$ curve, but gradually dampening in amplitude as it is bound by (enveloped) $y = \frac{1}{x}$.

5.2 Geometry

- When problems arise of the ratio of shapes with shapes, the usual scenario is circle/s in a triangle, the angles of the shape also have to be considered as well as the side lengths and/or radi of the shapes.

- A single circle inside an equilateral triangle:

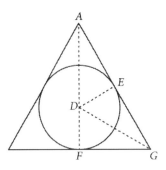

Rules:
1) $AF = 3DF$
2) $AF = \frac{\sqrt{3}}{2} AG$
3) $\sin 30 = \frac{DF}{DG}$
4) $\cos 30 = \frac{FG}{DG}$

5.3 Statistics

- Basic statistics is usually questioned, your knowledge does not need to surpass Additional Maths (if taken at GCSE). The common questions that come up require forming tree diagrams.

- Tree diagrams look at the probability when multiple events are considered.
e.g. The probabilities on any branch must total to one. You multiply along the branches to calculate the probability of that branch occurring. For example a box contains 4 black and 6 red pens. A pen is drawn from the box and it is not replaced. A second pen is then drawn. Find the probability of:

(i) two red pens being obtained.
(ii) two black pens being obtained.
(iii) one pen of each colour being obtained.
(iv) two red pens given that they are the same colour.

Draw tree diagram to discover:

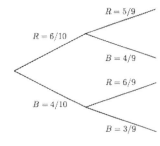

(i) $\mathbb{P}(\text{two red pens}) = \frac{6}{10} \times \frac{5}{9} = \frac{30}{90} = \frac{1}{3}$.

(ii) $\mathbb{P}(\text{two black pens}) = \frac{4}{10} \times \frac{3}{9} = \frac{12}{90} = \frac{2}{15}$.

(iii) $\mathbb{P}(\text{one of each colour}) = 1 - \frac{30}{90} - \frac{12}{90} = \frac{8}{15}$.

(iv) $\mathbb{P}(\text{two reds} \mid \text{same colour}) = \frac{1/3}{1/3 + 2/15} = \frac{5}{7}$.

- Conditional probability looks at a probability given an event occurs e.g. P(second pick is a red pen | first pick is a blue pen) = 6/9.

- Permutations: The number of different ways of selecting r objects from n when the order of the selection matters is given by: nPr. It can be calculated by:

$$nPr = \frac{n!}{(n-r)!}$$

- Combinations: The number of different ways of selecting r objects from n when the order of the selection does NOT matters is given by: nCr. It can be calculated by:

$$nCr = \frac{n!}{r!(n-r)!}$$

5.4 Circles

- Equation of a circle is given by:

$$(x-a)^2 + (y-b)^2 = r^2$$

Where r = radius, and (a,b) is the centre.

5.5 Calculus

- Methods of integration from all of the core models should be known. Some of the more complex examples are below:

- By substitution: If there is a function and its derivative in an integral a substitution of u=f(x) can be used. For example $(u = cosx)$:

$$\int tanx\,dx = \int \frac{sinx}{cosx}dx = \int \frac{-du}{u} = -ln|u| + c = -ln|cosx| + c$$

- By parts:

$$\int uv'dx = uv - \int u'vdx$$

- Methods of differentiation from all of the core models should be known. Differentiation is generally more straight forward than integration.

5.6 Binomial Expansions

- Maclaurin expansions are useful, but not required to answer questions. the general binomial expansion:

$$(a+b)^n = a^n + nC1(a)^{n-1}(b) + nC2(a)^{n-2}(b)^2 + ... + nC(n-1)(a)(b)^{n-1} + b^n$$

5.7 Inequalities

e.g.

$$5 - 3x < \frac{2}{x}$$

To solve this inequality, the fraction must first be removed, since x could be negative it is best to times both sides by x^2 so that signs do not matter, then solve the resultant quadratic. Factorise first, then draw a graph and select the appropriate region to solve.

Chapter 6

Visit our Website

https://oxfordpat.haptoid.co.uk